PARABLES

from

SHAMBHALA

PARABLES

from

SHAMBHALA

*The Wisdom of the East
for Everyday Life*

ZINOVIA DUSHKOVA

Radiant Books
Moscow

Note on language: To refer to a human being of any gender, this book uses the word *man*, which has its roots in the Sanskrit *manu* ("thinking creature"), and the pronouns *he*, *him*, and *his* accordingly. This is not intended to exclude women, but simply to ensure readability and clarity, since gender-neutral language can sometimes be cumbersome and confusing.

Publisher's Cataloging-In-Publication Data

Names: Dushkova, Zinovia. | Gerasimchuk, Alexander, translator.| Lvova, Natalia, illustrator.
Title: Parables from Shambhala : the wisdom of the East for everyday life / by Zinovia Dushkova ; translated from the Russian by Alexander Gerasimchuk ; illustrated by Natalia Lvova.
Other titles: Kniga pritchei. English
Description: Moscow : Radiant Books, 2016. | "This book was originally published in Russian as *Kniga Pritchei* by Zadruga, Kiev, in 2006."
Identifiers: ISBN 978-5-9905431-6-4 (paperback) | ISBN 978-5-9905431-2-6 (e-book)
Subjects: LCSH: Spiritual life—Parables. | BISAC: BODY, MIND & SPIRIT / Inspiration & Personal Growth.
Classification: LCC BL624.D8813 2016 | DDC 204/.4—dc23

British Library Cataloguing-in-Publication Data

A catalogue record for this book is available from the British Library.

Published in 2016 by Radiant Books,
an imprint of Dushkova Publishing, LLC
www.radiantbooks.org

ISBN 978-5-9905431-6-4 (pbk)
ISBN 978-5-9905431-2-6 (ebk)

Contents

Publisher's Note

Shambhala is a legendary kingdom hidden in the Himalayas, known under different names in the myths and beliefs of various peoples of the world: the City of Gods, the Garden of Eden, the White Island, and so on. It is the sacral source of all religions, philosophies, and sciences. Therefore, the wisdom originating from Shambhala underlies not only Eastern belief systems but also Western, including Christianity.

It is known that prominent people such as Gautama Buddha and Jesus Christ visited Shambhala during their lifetimes. Anyone who visits this place by an invitation resonating deeply in their heart takes a vow of silence, which may be broken only with the permission of the Great Lord of Shambhala. Uninvited guests will never find the right way to reach this Paradise on the Earth owing to mysterious powers that guard it from any external invasions.

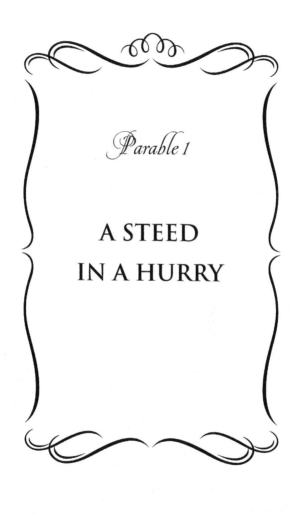

Parable 1

A STEED
IN A HURRY

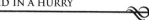

Stars faded and lit up again at the very moment when someone's invisible hand decisively drove away the cloud which was attempting to hide the vault of heaven with an impenetrable veil. And in the silvery stellar light illuming a mountain trail, there appeared a steed — persistently pushing forward, despite the fatigue attempting to fetter his flesh. It was as though he knew his goal and was sparing no effort in trying to reach it. And, notwithstanding his rider, who was immersed in a drowsy state, the steed continued to push forward, no one forcing him or spurring him on. The lifelessly dangling reins seemed as though they, too, were immersed in a dream, having surrendered themselves to the will of the hands that had held them tight with a strong and commanding pull — pointing out the path the steed was to pursue.

Who could show the right direction, then? Perhaps someone's invisible hand was pointing out the course to follow, or perhaps the steed was intelligent enough to be guided by the pattern of the stars. Nobody actually knew, for the world

was immersed in the dream, and only the measured pit-a-pat of pounding hoofbeats disturbed the silence of spheres mutely caressed by the silvery stellar light.

The four-footed pilgrim was striding confidently, despite the fact that he had not climbed mountain trails before. But that was not important, because he fully trusted his rider, knowing that he had only to stumble slightly and the horseman would immediately come out of his dormant state and pull on the reins in the blink of an eye to adjust the steed's pace and direction. Horse and rider seemed to merge with each other into a single whole. Thus, it was possible to afford rest to the man aloft, who, after gaining strength during his four-footed friend's repose, would help free the latter from fatigue — he would water and feed him, scour his coat plastered with road-dust and mud by plunging him into the rushing waters of mountain streams, and carefully card his mane. And then the path would seem easier, notwithstanding the very steep slope. And who will still remember when and where their

collective journey had started, what valleys and plains it had traversed? What encounters — joyful or sorrowful — marked its passage? Where did they interrupt their joint progress with an overnight stay? And how long did it last, this deathly calm leading to completely forgetting the need to continue the journey? Again, no one could say, as each one was immersed in their own sphere. The rider dwelt in the realm of bright visions of stellar expanses inhabited by other worlds, and, being immersed in the spheres of unearthly dreams, he was sweeping ever forward with all his spirit. Possibly, in his haste to reach his goal, he also inspired a sense of swiftness in his four-footed friend, who at first glance seemed rather lonely in pursuing his night-time path.

Thus, the flesh and the spirit often stride through life merged together. For the one without the other does not have the significance that is inherent in their union. The body without the spirit is dead, like a wild-grazing steed, never bridled nor guided on a long journey by a strong but caring hand. What can a sphere limited by

nothing but wild prairies offer? A search for better pastures? And the only goal is... the struggle for survival? And is it by sheer luck that it does not fall under the power of the sharp fangs of ubiquitous predators who tirelessly pursue the trails of prospective victims?

Yes, the body without the spirit is dead, for otherwise it is destined to move but in a vicious circle. But what is the spirit without the flesh? It is a horseman without a horse. Of course, he can achieve his goal, but will he have the time to reach it within the time allotted? How long will his way lie through rocky trails? This is where he needs a loyal ally. And only one who is also on this path can fill this role. So two companions come to light sharing a single purpose that can only be achieved though their merging. One provides the other with the path towards itself. And the spirit descends into the depths of the impenetrable spheres manifested by dense flesh. And there, in the darkness of Existence, is ignited the Light which affords the ability to behold the infinite possibilities of ascension, formed by the

rungs of Immortality. And the flesh, inspired by the vision, is invited into the realm of the spirit, to take a step into the boundless depths of the Stellar Ocean. Thus, the two poles, through their merging and the interpenetration of their fires, blend together as a single life-force, already taking up a unified position. And so are born the fire-breathing cores, created by opposing fires from the multitude of pros and cons that had been concealed within their depths. Everyone contributes their share in bringing about the formation of this fundamentally new power. And when it emerges into the light as a mature fruit, then yet another star blazes up in the vault of heaven.

...The steed is in a hurry. He needs time to reach his goal before the last star fades away — the Morning Star. After all, no sooner does it melt and the first rays of the Sun burst forth, than the time comes for his rider to wake up. And the steed does not want to part with him, knowing that it is within the rider's power to abandon his steed and choose a faster mount instead. The steed cannot betray his fatigue or reveal that a negligibly small distance has been covered. After all, this might well lead to his spending the remainder of his days in the stable. Who would wish to saddle up an old nag?! But if he demonstrates efficiency, then no rider will want to part with a good steed — on the contrary, he will take care of him in every possible way, restoring the forces lost along the path of life. And no traveller equipped with a faithful companion will want to get rid of him. Indeed, he will not ride a steed to death, who has trouble traversing the most steep and difficult segment of the journey.

Thus, one should always remember the wise interflow of life-forces so as to accelerate the pace towards a single goal, even when one does not know all the stops along the way. And when the goal is clear, all the surrounding spheres begin to offer their support throughout the path. And the Invisible Hand will take away all clouds, revealing stellar beacons to one's eyes. And the spirit will never know stops along the path, as it penetrates ever more deeply into infinite spheres, for

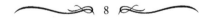

it will find a reliable foothold forever manifested in the soaring fires of the transfigured flesh. So, the steed in a hurry will appear as good Pegasus, spreading wide his luminous wings with the feathering of stellar rays, taking up half the sky. And he will take the Pilgrim of Eternity away, ascending towards the boundless peaks of his own transfiguration. Yet does not the tired steed, persistently winding his way upwards amidst rocky trails, see the same picture the rider sees in his state of dormancy?

Everything is possible, therefore the parable of the steed in a hurry is composed with a view to hastening him on, so that he may pursue his way keeping pace with his eternal companion — one predestined to be his fellow-traveller by Eternity itself.

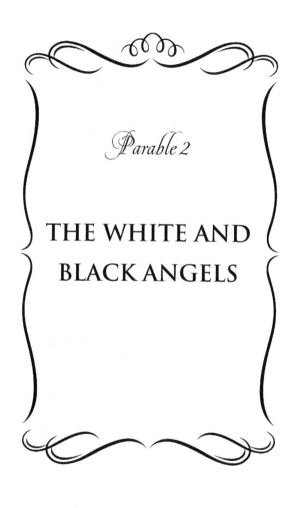

Parable 2

THE WHITE AND BLACK ANGELS

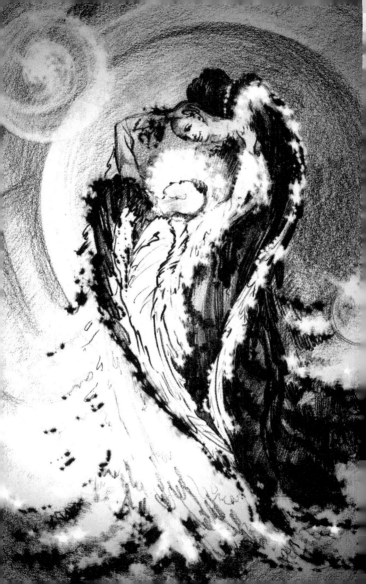

*T*wo Angels were moving towards each other. And, notwithstanding that they had set out from the opposite parts of the world, the direction they were heading in meant that their paths must cross. The White Angel was apparelled in shining garments woven from stellar light — garments blazing like the Sun — and wherever the foot of the Angel trod, their ineffaceable trace would remain and a spring would break through, pouring forth luminous streams into the world. The Angel coming towards him, by contrast, was Black, and his garments were as though woven from the fibres of impenetrable darkness. And why they were walking towards each other, only Heaven knows.

Indeed, the closer they got to the point where the two roads intersected, a number of things started happening which seemed weird at first glance. The garments of the White Angel seemed to be losing their original blinding brilliance, and with each step his strength was melting, left behind in the spheres he had already passed through. And now the dust of roadside fields began to leave its deposit, covering with a dense layer his luminous wings which hung heavily behind his back. Now the surrounding spheres started to fade in the twilight, for none other than the Angel himself had a source of fire capable of illumining them. But the garments became heavier and heavier — now they were already covered with a dense crust. Yet how could it be otherwise? After all, he was encountering dust, dirt, and impassable swamps along the way, and the White Angel could not pass around them, once he had chosen as his purpose to pave the shortest paths for ascending the rungs of his divine spirit. And now the goal is within reach: he is coming closer to here, to the point of the lowest descent. Here he must leave his luminous load so as to illumine the spheres of the "supreme" coagulation of darkness. But where is it and how can he see it, if it is dark all around and he himself has almost merged with the impenetrable spheres, composed of the countless abysses of Chaoses? And each succeeding step threatens to be the last.

In no way did the quiet footfalls of the Black Angel disturb the deathly silence of the realms immersed in gloom. He was not afraid to stumble, for he was already aware of all the traps that had been placed along the way. For a long time, the Black Angel had lived amidst the depths of the Chaoses, where his comprehension of the world of forms around him was not unlike that of a blind man. And the great number of falls he had experienced only served to teach him alertness, developing a hitherto unknown talent within his breast. So, the endless blows of fate ignited a whole host of sparks, allowing him to perceive accurate images all along the path of his advancement. Now a yearning for light arose within, compelling him to take swifter steps in his search for the source of the everlasting Fires. Yet was it not his heart-rending call that plumbed the depths of the abysses, all the way to the Light-bearing Spheres? And was it not the sensitive ear of the One Creator that had caught the whole pain of despair that had gone into this call? Perhaps it was He who had sent His Beloved

White Angel on a long journey, specifically to bring the Cup of Fire for the soul thirsting for the Light?

At this point the two Angels met. However, at the hour of their destined meeting both their garments were black. And there was nothing to illumine their way, for one of them, after magnanimously sharing his Fires with the spheres he had passed in the darkness, had only a tiny spark of life remaining in his sun-bearing breast. The other Angel had never known the greater light, but merely its momentary flashes, along with the anguish which had lain in his breast as a thirst for Fires, clenched in the jaws of darkness. How can one find the right path and lead along the trail of Light someone who has been blindly wandering in the darkness in search of the sun-bearing ways? And the White Angel decided to share his spark of life with the Black Angel so that the latter would be able to perceive the touch of Divine Fires, and thus fulfil the Behest of the Father of Eternity. So what did it mean that he himself, having lost the spark of life, would now merge with the surrounding darkness?! After all, the Black Angel had now found the path of salvation, which means the White Angel will find it, too, through sacredly preserving the memory of the Light-bearing Spheres. And, having decisively opened wide his breast, the White Angel breathed his spark of life into the breast of the one whom he had been called to save. All at once everything around was bathed in light — a miracle of transfiguration came about, and the Black Angel began to shine in snow-white garments. But at the same time he understood that, following the example of the White Angel, he must now bring back the life-bearing fires and generously share them with the surrounding spheres. And, descending into the depths of unknown abysses, he was to share his last spark of life with one who, perhaps, was uttering a heart-rending cry muted in the depths of Chaoses. So, their ways parted, after being united only for a few moments at a single point in the Universe.

And what about the White Angel? Will he die without the spark of life? Of course not!

He will acquire a new quality, one hitherto unknown. Thus, those who give their own life for another will themselves become immortal, for the Creator of Eternity clothes them in new apparel, hidden in which is the quality of self-regenerating fibres. But of course the White Angel had no idea of this at the moment when he offered the Great Sacrifice, thereby making an act of great refraction of the Divine Fires. Thus, the spark of his life continues the path, submerging deeper and deeper, until the Spirit of Transfiguration in Light touches all the Black Angels and they, like he, after parting with their sparks of life, begin to retrace the path of the White Angel's footsteps, who has endowed them all with life amidst Light.

So let us not blindly judge those whom we encounter on our way, no matter how black their garments may be. Let us remember that, perhaps, having concealed a small spark of life in their breasts, they are now winding their way into the depth of Chaoses, "falling" precisely into those abysses where they are destined to descend as a Saviour. And they will follow the path of the White Angel until all the spheres are suffused with the Light. There they will live and create, clothed in stellar apparel — those who have risen from the abysses of Chaoses, having changed their black apparel to snow-white garments woven by eternal stars. Let it be so!

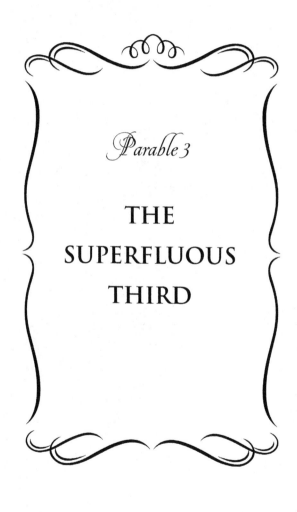

Parable 3

THE
SUPERFLUOUS
THIRD

*I*n one Empyreal Village there lived a youth who was noted ever since childhood for his great dreaminess. But nobody knew his dreams, because for the most part he was silent, keeping the world of his bright dreams away from the public eye. And each time he looked down from the Empyreal Heights at the lowlands immersed in gloom, he would try to find a wee flickering flame. It seemed to him that this was the soul of his beloved — a guiding star pointing the way to herself. Her allurement was so powerful that he could no longer content himself with watching her from a distance, and so decided to take to the road. However, he could not go down in the same apparel in which he soared amidst the Empyreal Heights. Where the darkness began, here, too, began the borders of a totally different world, beyond which one could pass only by putting on different garments. And whoever clothed themselves in human skins acquired a new status, and was now simply called — Man.

A man descended into the vale of tears and

grief. But his world of dreams, fixed in his breast since time immemorial, descended together with him. He was full of joy as he anticipated his meeting with his Only One — the One for whose sake his world had been founded, rejoicing as it did in the fires of its most daring dreams. Here a throne had been erected to which he would bring the queen of his spirit and lay the entire kingdom at her feet, presenting her with the sceptre of power for ages eternal. And may she hold sway over his heart, for there is nothing more beautiful on the Earth than the authority and power of Love. And when two hearts, merged together, beat only in the name of each other, then their power increases immeasurably, and they blaze forth as a single star, shining brightly throughout all space.

Long was the youth's path as he wandered from one sparkling little fire to another. Each time as he sat down by the fading fires, he tried to stir up the embers; but no sooner had they begun emitting their farewell warmth than they died out completely. You see, the fires had not been started for him, but were intended for other travellers, and, even as it showed them the path, a fire would joyfully blaze up more brightly when it detected the presence of the one whom it was specifically waiting for. Other fires would sorrowfully fade away, as the hand that had ignited the flame suddenly ceased feeding it. And the last embers died out along with fading human hopes. And then someone would set out, scattering the hot tongues of flame to the whims of fate, and, stepping into the impenetrable darkness, would head to a meeting with a long-awaited traveller. But how could one not lose a fiery beacon if the previous guiding light of a bonfire was suddenly snuffed out and only ashes remained? It is indeed difficult to follow a path without light, groping one's way through the thickets of darkness. Thus the youth walked on, refreshed only by brief respites, and being warmed, just for a few moments at a time, by the warmth of someone else's fire.

For the one who kept the flame of hope alive in her breast, the time of anticipation seemed infinitely long. She was waiting for the one who had appeared in her earthly dreams, igniting with an even greater force a multitude of unearthly reveries. The anticipation seemed to last forever, and there was no hope left to warm with its flame that very traveller in whose name she kept it burning through the night. And passers-by were certainly not averse to warming themselves during their own long journey of lonely progress towards the fires that were alluring them. And the flame of the bonfire, only barely aware of its own importance, would sadly lower its wings as it caught sight of yet another human spine retreating into the distance.

But where was *he*, the Only One? Which bonfires had he been detained by, caressed by someone else's warmth? Might he have forgotten the direction in which he was headed? Could it be that he had taken someone else's place and another had already passed by their goal, seeing it already occupied? And what if our young man saw another passer-by getting warm by the fire specifically intended for him and walked on past? Should he press on, seeking an alternative source of heat, or should he turn back? Perhaps he should defend his place and push aside the devourers of his own precious warmth? After all, there are those who, like parasites, are willing to live on the fruits of others' labours. And how many bloodsuckers there are who will never let go of their victims, latching on to them to the point of death!

Who is he in this world? Perhaps, he is a "superfluous third"? Hosts of bonfires are burning, but not in *his* honour does their flame rise. The only one shines its magically attractive light far off in the distance. But around it flicker shadows as well, signifying that nobody will yield to him his place by the fire. But is it not painful for her, the Only One, to waste her heartfelt warmth, sharing it indiscriminately with the throngs of passers-by? Is not the Flame of Life cultivated in the name of the One and Only Traveller? If swarms of midges fly towards the light, is the fire to blame? One little fly after another burns its tiny wings and falls into the fire. Yet is it to blame, if the fire's attracting power is too overwhelming for it? Indeed, payment is made at the cost of life.

So what is the reason to set out on a journey if you reach your desired goal only to do an about-face and completely miss the precious warmth? Why should you aim to reach the spot where you, the Only One, are being waited for? Why cultivate worlds, brimming over with the light of hope, if you cast away all your priceless dreams of Love, like pearls before swine? Why start bonfires that aimlessly collect nothing but midges? Why was life given to you, O Man — is it so you yourself can be a superfluous third, or, alternatively, so you can take your place occupied by someone who really is a superfluous third? And is it not you who are entitled to be the Only One when you appear before the eyes of your Beloved One?

What could be more important in the world than the fusion of two hearts whose flame has been ignited in the name of each other and has been burning perennially for millennia, thereby fulfilling the Mission of Love amidst the darkness of the earthly spheres! Love and Love alone creates the patterns of stellar destinies, igniting high bonfires in the breast of everyone who has reached out for her eternal warmth. She, having sown her seeds, reaps a ripe harvest, reared by her currents in the depths of human hearts. The Love of Love is irreproachable. Is it not she, as the Supreme Behest of Heaven, who puts everything in its place, like night-time luminaries, so that even at the greatest distance two kindred fires could blaze up with unearthly attraction, aspiring towards each other. And she alone — Divine Love — is privileged to understand the whole depth, manifested by the unification of two hearts, fire-breathing the light of each other. And who but Love knows how difficult it is to be a superfluous third, because she has been in anticipation of the reciprocal love of the Human Race for billions of years, inflaming the bonfires of ever new hopes.

And now her Time has come. She is in anticipation of the one who will bring her the flame of the greater Love. And they both will meet, attired in earthly raiment, appearing in the image of human beings, summoned to show an example of the Greatest Love. And once Love has settled inside the human heart, everything else is already superfluous, for the third always comes from the mind.

And what about the youth? He is on his way! And obviously Love will help him achieve the intended goal, appearing as a lodestar ahead of him. And when his mind gives the reins of government to the loving heart, then he will cease to be a superfluous third. And the sceptre of power over her heart will be put in his hands by her who has always anticipated the Only One, having freed herself from superfluous thirds for the sake of being the Only One for ages eternal. May the Sacrament of Fiery Unification be accomplished! Let it be so! Amen.

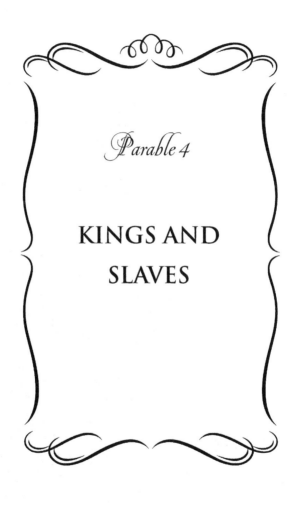

Parable 4

KINGS AND
SLAVES

*F*or some, white-stone palaces, embellished with magnificent decoration, are prepared; for others — gloomy hovels, cold and miserable in their appointments. And often in the former sphere of habitation live, oddly enough, slaves. They are enslaved in chains by a master named *matter*. Why is the power of materiality over human nature so strong and boundless? Is it because it represents colourful forms in abundance, helping to cover up the slavish soul, and now one robed in royal garments is perceived as a lord? Why does Nature act like that, ensconcing slaves on royal thrones while imprisoning free royal spirits in cramped hovels? Does not she have other worries than to amuse herself with permutations which, at first glance, cause not only bewilderment but also resentment?

How often does it seem to us in life that someone else is occupying our rightful place, unfairly wielding power over the territories under our jurisdiction! And we try to mentally control something or someone, attempting to apply our laws that in most cases turn out to be ineffective. Is it that slaves do not listen to kings or perhaps we are not kings? And often, upon encountering misunderstanding or rejection, we close in upon ourselves and obediently submit to circumstances, thereby positioning ourselves on a lower rung of a ladder hammered together from slavish principles. Who is it that Life wants to create from us? Whom does it need: kings or slaves?! Are not kings prone to be too proud and wilful? They will never submit themselves, like slaves, to something their spirit does not like. And then how can the Forces of Life cope with them? Would not it be easier to deal with slavish obedience? Who are we in fact? Does Creative Nature cultivate within us the seed of a king or a slave? And what, in fact, in her understanding, is a slave and what is a king? How close are we to understanding the essence of these two opposite creatures?

A King was born... And once upon a time the first sounds emitting from the breast of the new-born pervaded a white-stone palace. It seemed as though the heir was claiming his inviolable rights to his father's throne. Like distant thunderclaps, people felt the power of his royal spirit hidden deep within his breast, to which not only persons of royal titles may bow, but all the Forces of Nature.

Yes, here was born the King of Kings! So, it is he whom Divine Nature had been begetting in her womb for long æons on her path. The day marking the birth of the Heir was calm and cloudless. The world seemed to stand still in anticipation to hear something immensely important. And suddenly everything around began to speak. These were voices bursting through from the depths of the human breast. This was the beginning of a dialogue — here was speaking none other than the King of Kings, composing his silent speech from heart to heart. The voice, in which resounded all the shades of sound of the Divine Spheres, silently commanded kings to throw off their slavish fetters and to elevate their free spirit to its full height. The time allotted for testing the kings has passed. Thus, in voluntarily enchaining themselves, they were in fact testing the power of their royal spirit, submitting themselves to the slaves of their flesh. And the time allotted for testing the slaves has passed as well. After being brought into white-stone palaces and robed in royal clothes, will they be able to maintain the height of the position assigned to them and to establish themselves on thrones in the royal spirit?

The King of Kings has entered the world... And those who did not succeed in eliminating the spirit of slavery fled from off their thrones. The true rulers began to take their places, and Divine Nature herself, having started a game known only to her, began — like the last grave-digger — to rake up all the fallen leaves from the Tree of Life, burying the "spirit" of slavery under the heap of oblivion, as a phenomenon absolutely foreign to the Forces of Evolution. And what of the master named *matter*, whose reign had seemed so cloudless?! He realized that he himself was a slave of the forms he created. And therefore, having woven his attire from altogether

new fabrics, he brought it to the Spirit of the
King of Kings, thanks to which he was able to
descend into the World of Matter. Being a slave
to ourselves is the worst form of slavery, and re-
lease from the chains of slavery depends upon us
alone. Freedom — this is the destiny of kings. A
weak-willed submission to the power of a lower
creature — that is the destiny of slaves.

Divine Nature herself, on the other hand,
tests everyone to see who is a king and who is a
slave in their essence, regardless of how we wish
to identify ourselves. Either the king or the slave
can emerge within us and thereby give prepon-
derance to one pan of the scales over the other.
External wrappings are nothing; our internal garments are everything. And if a white-stone palace
is found within one's breast, it means that a king
of the spirit is manifest in the flesh. To be either a
king or a slave in bondage to slaves — this is your
choice to decide, but remember that the world
of the Earth has been released from the chains of
slavery, for the King of Kings has descended —
the Lord whom all the kings of the world

worship in the spirit. And whether you will have an occasion to meet Him, depends upon you, for you are forging your own path within yourself as you progress from slave to king. True kings do not like slaves, and so you ought to know that if you remain in slavery, you will deprive yourself of meeting Him, for He is destined to be, now and forever, surrounded only by kings of the free spirit and from everlasting to everlasting. Amen.

He had already come to slaves, but the slaves did not recognize Him. And therefore He has now come to kings...

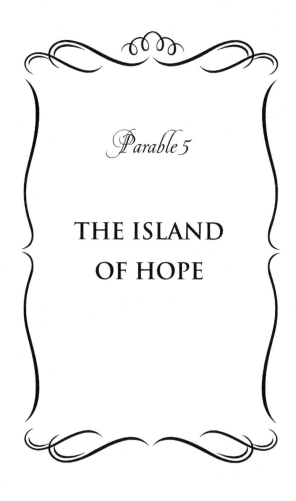

Parable 5

THE ISLAND
OF HOPE

aves are storming all around. They are full of the vital force that drives them to unknown shores. And both above and below the water, everything is in motion. Violent winds are wailing, tugging at the sails of ships exhausted from their arduous journey, hurrying towards a safe haven. One after another, bevies of fish flit past in pursuit of food or in an attempt to escape the jaws of a predator threatening to crunch them in its teeth. Life is teeming with all sorts of colours and sounds. And only an island, seemingly standing still amidst the raging waves, shows forth unwavering firmness. But is it really so lifeless as it appears at first glance?

Tireless toilers of the sea have scoured coastal stones till they are white. Waves incessantly wash the shores, occasionally displaying their gifts upon sands which the Sun has burnt out in white heat. And the island becomes "richer" with every new piece of flotsam and jetsam concealing an appeal within. However, it cannot move from its place to rush to answer a cry for help, because, like a watchman, it has risen above the waves, having been fixed in one place by an unknown someone's Hand. The island has its own destiny, described only in secret scrolls. And who knows what it conceals within its bowels: perhaps, innumerable treasures are hidden in its caves, or, perchance, a Bird of Happiness abides there, raising its nestlings in a sanctuary undisturbed. And then more than one Blue Bird of Happiness will appear in the world, and everyone who is hunting for it will be able to meet up with it. However, if they attempt to imprison it in a narrow cage, it will disappear on the spot, for Happiness cannot live in captivity.

Man is an Island. And its name is Loneliness. Around it is a sea of raging passions. And the waves that beat against its shores, are not they taking away a part of its outer fringe, thereby reducing its very borders? Do not storm winds of gigantic force break the crowns of trees whereon the Bird of Happiness could build its nest? And is not the "flesh" of the island, already withered by the heat, wounded by sharp-edged rocks? Further, the hidden treasures — are not they

the eternal target of robbers who live at the expense of their spoils? The island itself is mute, and therefore cannot emit a cry for help, or seal a message in a bottle and consign it to the will of the waves. And there is no cosy haven to attract the gaze of passing ships. Here amidst the stormy waves of life, it is not the island that chooses. Rather, it is chosen by those who wish to set their feet on dry land.

Of course, every island dreams of one day seeing Scarlet Sails on the horizon, borne by all the winds directly to its shores. And at the helm will be none other than the one who intended to visit this island in particular. But people often end up on the island as the result of a shipwreck, carried on pieces of wreckage as a "gift" from the sea-waves of life. And while it will accept this unexpected offering of destiny, the Bird of Happiness will not sing its song for them, for it knows that those whom the island rescues will always strive to leave it, using every excuse to press on to other shores. And this will only exacerbate the island's loneliness, compelling a more vigilant search of the distant horizon in anticipation of beholding a glimpse of the fabled Scarlet Sails.

High and implacable are the waves, as though they are arguing with each other, rising higher and higher. Who will spy this island, so small and inconspicuous in the massive mist of the raging elements? It cannot leave for the refuge of the mainland and find shelter there in a safe haven — such a haven, no doubt, is already full of seagoing ships, and there is no place for yet another. And to be driven away by the four winds, not knowing the purpose of your journey, not knowing where someone might be waiting to welcome you with open arms and where you could cast anchor — this is indeed an unenviable prospect. How many islands have already been drowned in the abysses of the seas of life! Still, after all, it is a *special* island, and it is unique in that it is capable of *waiting* — a quality inherent only in those who have the secret treasure named Hope. The price of this treasure is so high that one cannot buy it, even if one gave away everything concealed in the deepest reaches of all the gold-bearing caves

of the world. The island waits for someone who, firmly holding the helm, can overcome even the most "perfect storm" hiding from sight the shore of Hope — the purpose of every test of life. Such a one, knowing well their course, will never go astray and, having conquered hundreds of thousands of miles, will reach the shore of ultimate refuge — whose soil offers a firm foothold for evermore.

The island brims over with joy, shutting out any feeling of loneliness. Here it is Hope which spreads its invisible wings, growing more and more every day. And these wings, like sails, rise above the island itself. They are imbued with all the colours of life, showing themselves forth in a scarlet glow. All the sounds of existence are resurrected here. The island now lives exuding a foretaste of Happiness, for the Bird of Happiness has already made its nest here. This island is brimming with hopes, which, like nestlings being born every day to the light, spread the colourful feathering of their wings, proclaiming in song coming days woven from the Joy of Joys. Higher

and higher rise the Scarlet Sails, soaring far above
the raging waves of the sea of life. And now all
at once someone buried under shards of storm-
crushed ships catches a glimpse of the Scarlet
Sails, and feels the hope of salvation reviving
within them. And when one has hope, death has
no power over their hidden treasure. And someone will approach you and will lift you onto the
deck of the ship, allotting you a worthy place under the canopy of the Scarlet Sails. Indeed, if your
storm-driven boat cannot withstand the pressure
of destructive forces, the waves themselves will
inevitably carry you towards the shores of refuge. You need only manage to hold tight to that
which is ever unsinkable — to Hope.

Man is an island, and if he has even a drop of
hope, he deserves to be called an Island of Hope.
And even though today you bear the stamp of
loneliness, and storm winds are ready to tear your
still weak sails to shreds, do not ever let the invisible helm out of your grasp. Then you will be
escorted by all the forces of Nature, transported
on the crest of the waves to where someone is

waiting for you, cherishing the deepest of hopes for the destined meeting. And then, right there amidst the ocean of raging passions, your island will emerge and become the embodiment of the Indestructible Citadel. And so, after being washed by all the waves, caressed by the breath of winds and permeated by the rays of all the fire-breathing luminaries, you will discover the island of refuge not only for yourself but also for others who will be able to find salvation after being thrown overboard by the forces of destructive elements.

In this way, you can already today render assistance to Someone's Invisible Hand, which is ever creating new islands amidst the waves of the sea of life. And the mundane world will be enriched by yet another island, on the pattern of the original White Island, which rescues the souls sinking to the bottom of the ocean of passions of the whole Human Race. This indeed is the Island of Hope, which was established so that each of us who has been depicted as an island of loneliness, might rise as an island of refuge and

Hope, showing forth inviolable principles in the limitless sea of suffering human souls. Let it be so! Amen.

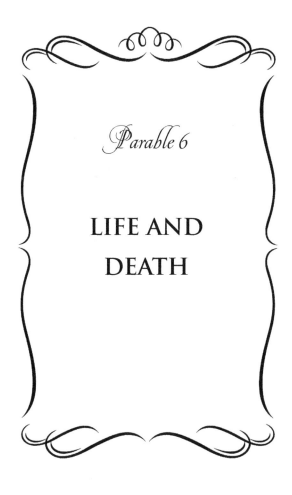

Parable 6

LIFE AND
DEATH

nce upon a time Life and Death met at the bedside of a seriously ill man. They stood one on the right side, the other on the left, staring intently at each other.

"Why did you come here?" asked Death.

"He called me!" answered Life.

"But he has never belonged to you!" objected Death, "As a 'living' person, he sowed only destruction and perdition, thereby faithfully serving me. See, his forehead is stamped with my seal. This is truly a man of Death! Go away, leave to me what belongs to me!"

However, Life was unwilling to yield the position afforded it by the call of the human soul.

"Whatever has a soul, concealing within itself the spark of Heavenly Fires, cannot belong to Death. That means you cannot take what is stamped with the seal of Immortality!" Life declared decisively.

The man was lying on his deathbed, surrounded by silence, and only the measured tick of a clock disturbed his deathly rest. But all at once he thought he could hear voices, and those quite close by. After listening more attentively, he realized that they were talking about him. It was as though he had become an unintentional witness to someone's dialogue. Indeed, to whom did he belong? Whose voice was closer to him? One of these voices was rude and authoritative, and its sounds increased the feeling of suffocation, as though someone were trying to tighten a noose around his neck. The other voice was decisive, but at the same time tenderly exhortative; its sounds had a most soothing effect, allowing its subject to take another deep breath. The one side blew a deathly, freezing cold while the other exuded a warm breath of living fire. As the man reached out to what had suddenly taken on the force of magnetic attraction, he began clinging ever so tightly to its life-giving currents.

"Well," said Death, "take his soul, but give me his flesh, for it is woven from my very threads — from the dust and ashes of the earth. Let us divide him in two, and we each shall have that part which belongs to us."

"I will leave the choice to the man!" Life

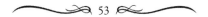

replied. "After all, the flesh is the garment of the spirit. And if the mortal's lips made their appeal to Immortality, how could I separate one from the other? Only man is free to decide whether to cast off his garments."

And right then the unexpected happened — the gravely ill man, having summoned the last of his strength, appealed to Death: "Take to yourself all that is perishable, for my soul is incapable of being adorned with garments of decay. I renounce all my vestments which have been put to the service of Death. I renounce you, my lord, whose only goal is the pathway to Death. And from here on in I appeal to the Forces of Life — may they grant me advancement as I climb the life-affirming rungs of Life's ladder! Let them send down that Death which comes in the name of the affirmation of Life! Let the Death they send down lift from our shoulders the burden of past years that is full of errors and bitter delusions leading nowhere! Let Death itself come down and reap its harvest! And as for such a harvest, which is entirely unsuitable for any further sowing, may it be handed back to Death, burying everything it owned under the heap of oblivion!"

"Death! Why did I see you as my enemy? I was afraid of you, and was not this the reason that I was slavishly trying to serve you?!" Thus mused the man as he climbed the path of Empyreal Ascent. "Death! It appears that you can be a loyal friend who frees me from an unliftable load. So, do you yourself not serve that omnipotent power which is simply called... Life?! Yes, it is possible to live only by dying!" the mortal man summarized his thoughts as he climbed the rungs of Immortality. He already knew that to ascend the next spiral of Divine Evolution he would have to die out of the life he had lived before. And life, once granted, can never be taken away; on the contrary, it bestows the right to be born again and again in a brand new state. And only Life itself is capable of knowing how many lives we can live over the course of a single brief human age.

We come from Nowhere and we go Nowhere. In the meantime, these are precisely the points where Life and Death intersect. These are their Gates, through which we pass upon the expiry of a specific period of Time. At the very moment when we are born, we fall under the power of Death, for within us hundreds of thousands of cells begin to die, having outlived the all-too-brief period allotted to them. Again, being subject to the breath of Death, we gain the power Life has over us. It gives rise to myriads of new cells, permeating them with its Life-affirming Force. So, do not we go hand in hand with both Life and Death throughout our entire lifetime? And is it only at our deathbed that they come into contact with one another for the first time, thus launching the eternal argument: To whom does this human being belong?

Here is a cradle magnificent in its adornment. And a newborn baby, peacefully sleeping, reposes therein. Nobody is around... But is that really true? Even while sleeping, the baby hears voices: one of them is authoritative, whereas the other is tenderly exhortative. They seem to be arguing as to which of them will lead this person through life, grasping firmly its wee hand limply placed in the palm of a Guide or, on the contrary, holding tight, apparently afraid of getting lost during its journey without parental care? The baby sleeps, and has dreams. Perhaps it is a human soul, enshrouded in tight swaddling-clothes of dense matter, and staying all too long in a slumberous torpor. After all, is not a dream akin to a little death, when the flesh lingers in a period of inactivity? Is this not why Death attempts to affirm its claims not only to the flesh, but also to the human soul, trying to extract something mortal therefrom which does not belong to Immortality? But will Life really lose all that much if Death takes away its own? On the contrary, Life will actually gain more, for the life-bearing seed will be freed from the suffocating chaff. And does not Life itself welcome the companion walking beside it in the name of Death?

Indeed, the whole mystery of Life and Death is concealed under seven seals and at the same time is revealed for all to see, because the key to its puzzle is none other than Man himself, being a point of refraction between Life and Death on the Earthly Plane. But still, one should always remember that Life is not conceived for the sake of Death, but Death is paving its Life Path for the sake of Life. And so it will be until the end of time! Amen.

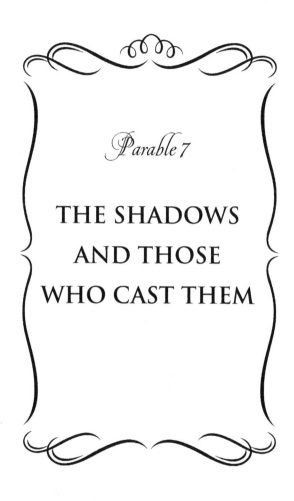

Parable 7

THE SHADOWS
AND THOSE
WHO CAST THEM

Can a shadow be without the one who casts it? Does it have a separate and independent life, entitled to produce its own actions, wandering just anywhere on a whim? Sometimes we observe our own shadow, finding amusement in the contemplation of the motions it synchronously produces. But have we ever given thought to just what this shadow is — does it have any degree of self-awareness, and, if it is endowed with a modicum of reason, what might it "think" about us? Who are we in its eyes? And why does it appear for the most part only when additional lighting — natural or artificial — is present? And why does it completely dissolve in the surrounding space when darkness sets in?

If the source of light is behind us, the shadow usually covers that which appears directly in front of us. Could it be that the shadow is trying to tell us something? And, when we turn to face the light, we lose this eternal companion, but then we behold the whole scene before us in all its clarity. Why is the life of our shadows so mysterious? What do they conceal within themselves? What do they consist of? It is said that one cannot step on someone else's shadow or even step over it. Why should this be? Perhaps it is an attempt to convince us that this makes us vulnerable to someone else's illnesses or can attract some other misery from a shadow cast by a sick or evil person. Perhaps this is how the human mind attempts to comprehend the mystery of shadows cast either by one's self or by one's fellows? Yes, *cast* is the operative word here. Perhaps, our flesh "exhales" or detaches a part of itself, which remains as an ineffaceable mark wherever its shadow has fallen at least once? With the multitude of mysteries in the world, how is it that one of them relentlessly follows us throughout our entire life, not leaving us even for an instant until man, or rather, our soul, finally casts off its whole dense attire — or, to be more precise, that which causes the shadow to be cast in the first place.

But is not the human flesh itself a mere shadow cast by the human soul? And, furthermore, is not the soul generated by the supreme spirit as its reflection? And perhaps the Kingdom of Truth is the Kingdom of Spirit, and everything else illuminated through the prism of the Divine Light is but the Kingdom of Shadows? But if the shadow with amazing accuracy reproduces the actions of the source that cast it, may not one assert that we are the continuation of the Empyreal Kingdom and therefore in our essence we have a single and indivisible nature? After all, there is no shadow manifested apart from man! And if the shadow of the spirit is the soul, and the shadow of the soul is the flesh, why cannot one continue this series of reflections and endue the shadow cast by the human flesh with some form of reasonable existence with its own secret meaning?

The spirit is endowed with the supreme property of sound, "crystallized" by the currents of Immortality. The soul, standing on a step below, is already endowed with the fiery consonance of a lesser power in relation to its spirit. So man is merely a shadow in relation to his soul, for often its supreme goals remain a mystery to the earthly mind. However, the soul knows for what reason

it has been robed in mortal garments, while man is still unaware why Nature has bestowed upon him a speechless shadow, following the path amidst the trails of life step by step together.

They say that if a human shadow falls on a stone, one can read, using special devices, all the information about the person who has passed by — even after thousands of years! How can people say that? Who puts such thoughts into their heads? But still they do say it, from one age to the next, thereby enriching the treasure-house of the Human Race with yet another little grain of knowledge that shines like a pearl, already casting its own shadow. And thought is so agile! And if even stones can cast their own shadows, why should not one ascribe a similar quality to thought? And is not this how shadows take care of themselves, casting their own shadows into the world around them, thereby silently giving voice to the innumerable tongues of Nature?

It is not man that follows shadow, but shadow that follows man. And that is how it was established from the very beginning, for the soul,

following the spirit, leads the way for human flesh. And someone unknown, whose Name is Mystery, guides our divine spirit. After all, gods themselves have Gods who lead them ever higher up the rungs of ascension, and these may well be unfathomable not only to the mind but also to the spiritual understanding. And as the spirals of Evolution go up, so one is obliged to notice the rungs going down, paved with great foresight by the Forces of Light. But our shadow can fall not only into the depth of petrified nature, but also into bottomless abysses which serve as the originating source of primordial elements. There, amidst lifeless spheres, Life conceives new forms of creation that, perhaps, will adorn newborn worlds billions of years hence.

Thus the developmental History of the Human Kingdom leaves its eternal trace, falling as a shadow into the spheres of the vital activity of the Animal Kingdom, which casts a shadow into the Vegetable Kingdom. It, in turn, falls into the Kingdom of Minerals, and so on, projecting itself ever lower into the domain of Microworlds. Here mature the seeds which, as they rise through the Æons, will unfold as Macroworlds, concealing within themselves myriads of emerging Cosmoses. What is the responsibility of man before his own shadow then, if upon the quality of its energy coloration depends the life not only of his comrade who steps over it, but also of the unfathomably vast Chain of Evolution of the whole Divine Creation?

Blessed be the one whose soul lives in accord with the spirit. Blessed is the man whose soul imbues all his thoughts and acts with spiritual purity. Blessed, too, is his shadow, for it will bring healing to everything touched by the reflection of his blessed flesh. Even animals will be happy to curl up at the feet of their benefactors, preferring the safety of their shadow, either visible or invisible. And a plant will grow faster, blossoming forth in luxuriant radiance. Even a stone will be permeated with the healing spirit. We breathe out what we have inside, and we reflect what we are in our essence. Thus, the alchemic formula of our shadow is wrought by our own hands. And our eternal companion will be the one whom we deserve. It is not without reason they say in the East: "Happiness accompanies a good man like his shadow." And if our fellow-travellers should bring us misfortune, did not we ourselves draw them into our surroundings by our own tenebrous consonance? Who is to blame if our shadow is thus programmed — to follow us forever?

Shadows disappear at noon on the equator. It is the peak of manifestation of the fire-breathing luminary at its zenith. And, in emulating such an example, we should illumine ourselves by our inner light so as not to follow too close at heel, treading on our own shadow, but not so distant that it lags behind, despondently stretching out flat. Light will reach out to light by the Law of Attraction, and our higher structures will descend along fiery rungs, casting their sun-fuelled shadows. And together with them will come into the world the concept of the *spiritualized shadow*. Then we will no longer live in the Kingdom of Shadows, but in the Kingdom of Truth, which,

thanks to the selfless devotion of our shadows, will not know a shadow, for that is where Eternal Noon reigns supreme. And who knows, noon may well be that eternal starting-point which periodically shifts the hands of the Cosmic Clock, predetermining new periods within which Time and Space arise and new shadows begin to appear in the world, but on a completely different level of the alchemic formula of Light, for life is granted to us by the Behest of Noon! Who knows what secrets we are still to approach in the attempt to unravel the eternal riddle that our shadow has been wrapping in mystery for ages — our silent witness and companion throughout our earthly journey.

So let the Light of Illumination fill your heart to the brim — a heart which has already penetrated the great secret: why our shadow persistently follows the flesh, led by the inviolable union manifested in the image of Soul and Spirit, merged for the single purpose of attaining the Empyreal Heights. And blessed be its path through ages eternal. Let it be so! Amen.

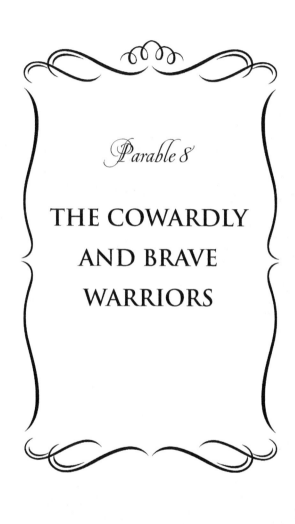

Parable 8

THE COWARDLY
AND BRAVE
WARRIORS

*L*ife is a battlefield. And all of us are warriors, either ready — to a greater or lesser degree — to confront all dangers face-to-face or opting to sit out in trenches while our brethren are defending their borders with might and main. There are even those who defect to the enemy, looking back with cowardice at the positions they abandoned — positions which they had sworn an oath to defend to the bitter end! And, by the same token, an enemy combatant may come over to us, having surmised the balance of power to be on our side. But what is the goal? Every warrior must have a clearly defined purpose, for the sake of which they are prepared to lay down their life on the field of battle. To throw oneself into the midst of an attack and pointlessly die in the name of someone else's aims — or rather, ambitions — is such a goal worthy of the warrior? After all, even warriors have only one life, and once they put on their armour, they do not sally forth in search of death, but to defend their right to life. At times, of course, circumstances may be such that death seems to be the only solution. And Life releases us into the arena of battle, allowing us like gladiators with weapons in our hands to win a few days or years more from Death, during which there will be incessant life-and-death clashes. Sooner or later, we shall have to show our military mettle and take our own place on the battlefield, for such are the conditions of Evolution, weeding out everything unsuitable for ascending its rungs. Yes, Life makes strict selections, but it *is* possible to understand it; otherwise, how will it continue if the strongest fail to survive? And so life criss-crosses the battlefield of everyday existence, marking those exhibiting the spirit of heroism with the seal of the chosen.

Where are the origins of bravery to be found? Where do warriors, having lost their strength in constant battles, draw new forces from? And where is the nature of cowardice to be fathomed? Where does this worm sit that gnaws away at human flesh? How many lives have been forfeited among troops led by cowardly commanders?! And how many souls have been saved thanks to the bravery of those who rushed into battle, diving right into the midst of the enemy host?!

Who are we? After all, there is a mass of people dependent upon our actions. Whom do we follow and where does the one who believes in us lead? The responsibility each one bears towards his neighbour is extremely great indeed. The earthly mind faces a countless number of ambushes. No sooner is it captivated by one path of ascent when suddenly it turns tail and heads in the opposite direction; not being happy with this, it dramatically takes its cue from a different marker, whereby it leads not only itself into an impenetrable thicket, but also any who thoughtlessly follow in its footsteps. Moreover, having reached an impasse, it abandons everyone to fate, attempting to find its own path of salvation — a path it had lost long ago. Death reaps an abundant harvest on the battlefield of life. And how can we not follow one who so eloquently describes the victory, easily attainable, and so relishes sharing a bearskin with others before killing the bear, promising fabulous trophies to boot?

Certainly this will make one's mouth water and the mind will gloss over with the glitter of fantasy-like treasures. And so the blind blindly follow their leader, unaware that many of them, already standing on the edge of an abyss, will find their eternal rest lulled under the wings of death. And is it not the abyss of insatiable greed that begets a pleiad of cowardly creatures helping to deliver bloodstained food? Do not the abysses of Chaos cover the planetary flesh with the web of cunningly tangled trails designated by a multitude of false markers? And, like the body of a giant snake, the densely churned mass of stray earthly children moves down black serpentine roads, being hurried along by sighted guides blindly carrying out the will of the Lord of Tartarus.

However, beacons of salvation often light the way, ignited by the Lord of Eternity. They point out the direction towards paths of salvation, and those who have not lost the alertness of the heart's eye will always be able to turn into such a path, carrying with them anybody who has maintained a craving for the Divine Light.

The source of bravery is inexhaustible. And it is not necessary to set out on a long journey in search of the life-giving force. It lies within us — as a luminous spark, resting in the human breast. Someone will grow this little sprout of flame, and it will appear as a fire-breathing glow at the hour of the decisive battle. But leave it to some coward to trample down the sparklet of light, so as not to offer a target to the enemy midst the darkness of the surrounding spheres. What they do not know, however, is that, along with the spark, they will trample down their own vital forces, thereby destroying themselves without even engaging in their first battle. We are all warriors, and the battlefield often unfolds within our own breast. The mind contracts in cowardice, attempting to find a way out, mentally declaring: "This is no concern of mine!" The heart, by contrast, attempts to shift human nature away from the deadpoint, forcing one to launch a decisive attack against any positions which, despite being outmoded, continue to apply a death grip and hold their victims hostage to ancient dogmas and prejudices. Man thus becomes his own hostage, having convinced himself that any step towards something new means betrayal of something already created. He is always afraid of betraying someone: himself, or others, and so on. Man must always look good in his own eyes. And the subconscious fear of "falling in his own eyes" pushes him to accumulate thoughts of doubt that swarm in the bowels of a wayward mind like a ball of snakes. In turn, thousands of excuses will obligingly be provided whereby someone with a cowardly soul tries to portray themselves as an incredible hero. But life cannot be deceived — it sees everything and allots a place to everyone according to the actions it beholds.

Of course, we can think anything we like about ourselves, imagining ourselves, for example, as a great commander, whose name alone is enough to make our enemies tremble in fear. But only the field of battle brings to light reality, as opposed to the product of a deluded imagination. Indeed, those who revel in illusions of their own fantastic bravery may well be the first to flee as cowards from an actual field of battle. And those who consider themselves lacking in heroic spirit may prove the bravest in practice, never letting the banner of victory slip from their grasp, resolutely hoisting it above the defeated foe's fortress. Walls deemed unassailable will collapse, solid enemy encirclements will break up, and the surrounding spheres will ring with the cry of triumph — only trust your own heart of flame, making it your Leader for ever. It truly knows the shortest paths to victory. The human mind is so afraid of defeat that it holds in a death grip even positions it has already conquered. It prefers "a bird in the hand to two in the bush." But, still, it is a "winner"!

How often in life, upon reaching a certain plateau, we stand stock still, satisfied to rest on our laurels that seem to be eternal! Certainly, no one is out to snatch away our past achievements. However, what if a gladiator with at least one triumph behind him is faced with the task of defending his title in yet another arena of life? Can you simply explain to attacking predators that you already have your recognition? As long as evil exists in this world, we have to be fully armed and claim our right to life every moment! And is it not for this that our souls, clad in the armour of solid bodies, are thrust into the arenas of life's battles? And we are compelled to fight strictly according to rules as defined by the Laws of Evolution. We cannot hope for our conquering foe's mercy, for there are only two alternatives: *life* and *death* — a third is not given.

A critical time has come. And the entire Human Race is brought to the Stage of Life, and, divided as it is within itself, it must determine a victor on the field of battle. Will Light or darkness finally hold sway? Will humanity show incredible bravery or leave the scene of battle like a coward? And the unifying Law of Life, like a conqueror sitting on the throne, will show forth a sign, either rendering supreme honours to the winner or handing the sceptre of power to Death to complete its task. What will the Human Race say? It will give an answer which each of us will demonstrate today on the battlefield, in mortal combat with ourselves! Indeed, as the ancient wisdom says: "Each man is his own best friend, and his own worst enemy!" And God grant that he will not be an invader, but a Warrior-Liberator, who has come to free his spirit for new feats of arms.

The Army of Light is amassing, permeated with the Spirit of Heroism, and each one of us has their place there. So let us not allow our Commander, represented by the image of Eternal Life, to find anyone missing among us. Let it be so! Amen.

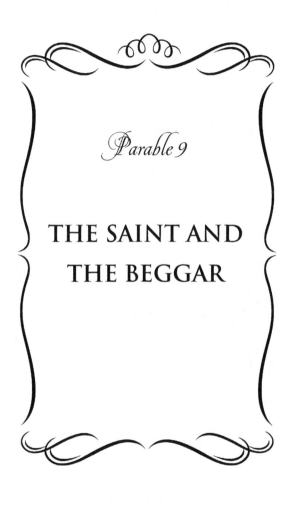

Parable 9

THE SAINT AND
THE BEGGAR

nce upon a time, as a pilgrim was walking through a forest, he lost the trail and went astray. Which way to go? Now the dusk was deepening, snatching away any hope of catching even the slightest sign that he was on the right path. The trees stood immersed in silence, and there was not even a small breeze to stir them. And only the rare sound produced by the forest's nocturnal inhabitants managed to reach the pilgrim's ears. Somewhere nearby a twig crackled, causing him to shrink in fear. Indeed, the forest is full of dangers, especially at night. Darkness is often the best ally for those in pursuit of their next victim. Why was the pilgrim going through the forest? All alone and without a guide, how could he be sure that he would reach his goal by the shortest path and spare himself so many additional days of travel? In the past his journeys had so often taken him by roundabout ways that, one could say, whole years had been spent on pointlessly weaving a winding way along the countryside's twisted trails. Moreover, he had worn out dozens of pairs of shoes treading those endless roads. So this time he decided at last he would reach his goal not by the back trails, but by selecting the most direct route possible. And what now? He paused in confusion in the midst of a forest thicket, encircled tightly by night-time shadows as well as by sounds which seemed to be menacingly approaching his position.

Where was he heading, this hapless pilgrim? What goal did he have that forced him to choose such a dangerous part of the path? Why was it so enticing that he did not want to waste even a moment in his haste to achieve it? The subject of the pilgrim's quest was simply... *Happiness.* He had been seeking it for his entire life, but the years had merged into decades and slipped away, bringing him no closer to his desired goal. But the pilgrim firmly believed that somewhere there must be a happiness specifically for him; he just needed to find and follow the right path. Otherwise, why had he been born? It was definitely not to waste his life in fruitless pursuit of illusive goals! The pilgrim firmly believed that man was born for happiness, and that without it life is simply meaningless. Only happiness can offer a feeling of fullness, and without it he was simply a beggar! And so here he was, treading his life-path like a beggar with a bag on his back. Approaching yet another little light promising deliverance as it flashed away in the distance, he was hoping to finally end up in the arms of people who would gladly embrace him like a long-awaited guest. Perhaps, it is here that his happiness was patiently lying in ambush, waiting to witness at last the attainment of his goal. But, alas! He was not even admitted past the threshold, and only crumbs fell onto his outstretched palm. So he made his way through life, being content with someone else's "handouts" while his own bag was still empty, for he still had seen neither hide nor hair of his expected happiness. And what was he without it? Just... a beggar!

O how many beggars are to be seen wandering earthly roads! But are all of them seeking Happiness? Some may be glad for even a crust of bread tossed to them — the way one might throw a morsel to a dog? And they will even feel

honoured to lick their master's hands and, obse-
quiously tucking tail, will hide under the table,
waiting for their stellar hour: "Maybe a gnawed
bone will fall to my lot!" Oh, these do not consider themselves beggars! Where should they go,
if, having curled up at the door of their master,
they feel they are already happy? Why should
they wander about like a homeless dog?

Yes, some need very little, others will not be
satisfied no matter how many food-plastered ta-
bles, luxuriant feather beds or granaries full of
corn they possess. These will leave their home —
an already overflowing cup — and set out for
a long journey, simply because nothing pleases
them if happiness is absent. Now one might be
curious as to what this Happiness looks like.
How can one recognize it and not pass by it
unnoticed? After all, it is not exactly a "known
quantity." And Heaven forbid one might blindly
remove oneself from the scene altogether, in
which case the journey back to Happiness might
well last longer than a human lifetime! But, you
see, someone else's happiness is no good to us,

because we cannot possibly be happy with a happiness that does not belong to us. Not only that, but if we try to seize someone else's happiness, we shall only multiply the misfortunes of the world.

Here the forest began to thin out and pre-dawn shadows began to disappear, exposing the trunks of leafy trees. How wonderful that the pilgrim had in no way been frightened by the roar emitted by the pitch darkness, but had resolutely continued on his way towards his goal, fending off all fears of the night! And then, all at once, his ears caught wind of a strange singing. As he headed in the direction of the alluring sounds, immediately the trees parted, as by the wave of someone's hand, revealing a vista over a beautiful meadow. Right in the middle of it was a hermit, sitting, as it were, on a carpet of flowers tightly encircling him. It was the brightest carpet the pilgrim had ever seen — a living carpet that simply effused fragrance, its magnificent flower buds seemingly beckoning him to sit down on the carpet. And at long last he stood still, interrupting a journey which had lately seemed to have cost him his last strength. The hermit was singing a hymn, his gaze fixed on the rising Sun. He was glorifying the rays of the Happiness-bearing Orb. The pilgrim tried to peer into the multitude of the luminous rays directed towards him, but he still could not discern in them anything that might be described as Happiness. And then, all at once, he felt something stir within him, something he had not felt before. As though the dawn itself were taking birth within his breast! Moreover, it was stretching its luminous feathers, spreading a caressing warmth through every cell of his exhausted human nature.

"O Lord! How happy I am!" the man said to himself quite unexpectedly. And truly at this very moment he felt within himself: "Here it is, Happiness! I have found it! How many roads I had to travel, spending dozens of years of my life to find my Happiness. This is its home, and this is the light I should have followed all along — it is my own heart! The eternal haven was in my very own breast! Why was I searching for it in other people's houses?" Meanwhile, it seemed, the currents of the rising Orb had spread across the whole breadth of the horizon. And the song of the hermit gave way to the living chirruping of birds. The pilgrim kept standing there, quite in awe of his discovery. Yes, his encounter with Happiness was indeed a revelation. How could he keep it within his grasp? After all, having manifested itself as a fire-breathing Orb and reaching the zenith of its glow, it was now free to set beyond the horizon. The pilgrim did not want to part with the wealth of feelings it was giving him! "O Lord, how rich I am!" he declared. He clearly felt an inner fullness, and this state of delight was ever growing, about to overflow the cup and, spilling over the edge, to illuminate with its breath the entire meadow and forest and, like the fresh breath of a breeze, to dash off into the vast expanses of infinity. Yes, in that case he could meet with his Happiness anywhere in the World.

"And what was the hermit doing in the meadow?" the question flashed through the pilgrim's head. He turned to the place where the song had rung out just moments ago, but saw no one. "Did I imagine it all?" he thought. And suddenly, in amazement, he found himself sitting on the carpet of living flowers, with hands outstretched towards the rising Sun. And his lips were already quietly singing a hymn, glorifying the rays of the Orb that had bestowed upon him the long-awaited meeting with Happiness. And he was happy to be a witness to the Happiness of the Sun: that Orb brimming over with Happiness was pouring it over the world in a flood, every ray pointing out the place where this sacred offering should be delivered. And there a sparklet had already been ignited, concealing the currents of Happiness within itself. And perhaps someone deprived of their own happiness could collect these luminous crumbs scattered throughout the earth and fill up their beggar's bag. Thus they would gain more strength along their way until they acquired their own Happiness.

The path of wanderings paved from ourselves to ourselves is indeed long, and often we set out on a lengthy pilgrimage in search of something we already have in our hands. But how many misfortunes, it seems, we need to meet on our way to understand a simple truth: Happiness lives within ourselves! It simply waits to meet us. So let us not walk on past it, since we already know that "one cannot build one's happiness on someone else's misfortunes"; moreover, it is equally true that one cannot build one's happiness on *another's happiness*, unless it is someone's kind offering to us, like the gift of the Sun.

The pilgrim came out of the forest and plunged into the network of earthly roads, full of wandering beggars. He handed them no crumbs of dried bread, but gave them something much greater — something that would not only compel them to throw off their beggarly rags but make them the richest people in the world. Like the rising Sun, the pilgrim himself marched to the zenith of manifestation of the fires of the heart, allowing the happiness of giving to grow with every gift.

He paid no attention to what his beneficiaries did with the gifts — whether they tossed them aside in favour of a brass farthing or pressed them to their heart, giving a powerful impulse to the awakening of their own fires. For the pilgrim it did not matter, because he was moving along a clearly designated orbit of advancement, never dawdling even for a moment.

He was following a true beacon — the Sun, whose luminous path he was determined to apply to his own life. And wherever his feet stepped, it was as though a ray of light were illuminating the pitch-black darkness, giving the opportunity to souls lost amidst the jungles of earthly paths to finally behold the light of salvation. And those who approached him felt as though the dawn of a new life were awakening within their breast, promising the Happiness of heaven. And people were now waiting for him, and upon meeting him would say: "Behold, the Saint comes to us!" Whereupon he, lifting his gaze towards the Sun overflowing with Happiness, would respond quietly: "You are — the only Saint, eternally leading us towards Happiness — the Happiness of knowing ourselves!" And who knows what paths we should take that we, too, might turn our eyes towards the Sun and say: "O Lord! How happy I am!"

Both the beggar and the Saint live within us. Whether we eke out a miserable existence leaving the treasure of our spirit unopened, or whether we take away all seven seals and open it wide, thereby immeasurably enriching not only ourselves but the whole world around us — depends upon us alone. Is it not better to traverse the orbit of our life path like the Sun, flooding the entire world with life-creating warmth so that it need never know poverty for ages eternal? Nothing can be compared with the wealth of your soul, Man of the Earth, for you are an Eternal Pilgrim, who has undertaken to carry the Cup of Heavenly Happiness unspilled, bringing it to the lips of everyone cherishing it and blessing every beggar, satiating them with Fires. Let it be so! Amen.

Parable 10

THE GOOD AND
EVIL TIMES

What is time like: good or evil? Someone may say: "Bad times have come," and everybody nods their head in agreement. "At last, evil times have passed," another sighs with relief. "Yes, it's true," still others chime in. It would seem that every day is born in the same way: the Sun always rises in the East, and whether the face of the sky is cloudy or clear — the Orb never strays from its own orbit of progression, bearing with it the same bright rays. Could they ever be filled with evil power, if they always give us life-bearing warmth? However, even the Sun has opponents. Pilgrims, for example, making their way through a desert, may find it hard to maintain a friendly attitude towards rays scorching them with merciless heat. They would prefer, in effect, to see a friend in a thundercloud hanging heavily over the red-hot sands. Others, by contrast, tired of incessant rains and surveying their crops crushed by hail, will give a heavy sigh and pray to the heavens to clear up the dome of the sky. And the hard times will pass, and once more the Sun will hide behind the horizon or spread its rays in a dawn of serenity, depending on who expects what from it. And so, bearing within themselves either good or evil gifts, the days and nights march around the earth, blending into a single concept — *Time*.

Time has power over everything. Yet people themselves seem to endow it with supernatural power, saying: "Time will tell," "Time cures all," "Time will come and put everything in its right place," and so on. They are often afraid of the return of old times, but even more often they live in fear, scared of anything that new times can bring them. Indeed, what colouring does Time have, and how can it have the ability to "return" if the hands of the clock are always dashing ahead? Perhaps, the secret lies in the clock face, which always forces the hands to move in a circle, despite the fact that they keep running only in one direction — forward? How can one fathom the mystery of Time, or at least open one of its facets even just a crack? One cannot catch Time or stop its run; it will still go through its changes day and night even when our own biological clock has

suddenly stopped, having counted out the period of time allotted to us. In fact, Time does not care in the least whether we exist in this world or not. It does not stop just because we stop and it does not follow in our footsteps. But if it is so indifferent to us, why do good and evil times so often change places in our life? And why do the good times, having barely flashed on the horizon as the first rays of reviving hopes, all of a sudden hide under the veil of gloomy thunderclouds, bringing us evil times? Where is that secret key whose turning affords us control over Time, capable of dispersing the menacing clouds hanging over the horizon of our life? But alas, for the time being it seems that man does not hold sway over time, but Time holds sway over man.

The measured tick-tock of the clock, like an experienced guide, leads us through the invisible pathways of Time. And we follow it obediently, close on heel, entrusting our own destiny to its footsteps. Perhaps it will lead us to a brighter future, one which we have imagined in our boldest dreams, and perhaps it will reward us with good times surpassing even our most daring hopes. But what if we find ourselves still in the same place where we started? Or even worse, what if we turn up at the epicentre of the worst times that have ever befallen us in all our born days? "How far can we trust Time?" that is the question. How can we determine whether friend or foe is manifest in its face? All it has to do is to warm us a little bit, and we immediately open ourselves wide, while if it pours cold over us, we closet ourselves away, utterly losing confidence in its power for good.

Yet still in the depths of the heart, a vague hope may glimmer that one day good times will come our way again. As day changes to night and night gives way to day — so here, too, the shroud of gloom will be dispelled and a new dawn will begin to blaze, impressing upon us that Time is not as indifferent to us as it first seemed; on the contrary, it was just testing us, wishing to determine how worthy we are of the gifts it has stored in its treasures especially for us. Yet has not Time prepared a Stellar Hour for us, serving as a loyal guide, leading us specifically to the zenith where the best time in our life becomes manifest? And the measured tick-tock of the clock is simply an indicator of how much progress we have made towards the ultimate goal, which has prepared a triumphal march for us, since from here to eternity our ally will be the omnipotent Lord, known to us under the name of *Time*.

Time — is immortal, for it lives in Timelessness. It allots a portion of its own time to us, restricting it by the limits of our human life. And where can Time lead us but to Timelessness? Perhaps the latter represents a different kind of clock face, whereby Time moves eternally forward through an immensely giant circle of its own manifestation. And these circles will form the fire-breathing coils of the unifying spiral of Divine Evolution. There can no longer be evil times once we know already here that Time is favourably disposed towards us and therefore it cannot do us wrong. And what we call bad times is merely a series of trials that we are to pass with honour, keeping within the period of time strictly allotted for this. So, let us believe that Time is a good healer, it will cure our wounds that we have endured throughout our long journey — either from our own lack of knowledge or the ignorance of our fellow-travellers. And Time will put everything in its proper place, having prepared a better destiny for us, as long as we keep pace with our guide, who is leading us towards Immortality by the shortest possible paths.

Time, too, has its time allotted to it for a test by Eternity itself. Timelessness tests it as a disciple climbing up the rungs of mastery of the Secret Wisdom. And so there are times when Time apparently ceases to exist, submerged in a state similar to death. And the Pralaya of Time — the Rest which is similar to a dream — lasts again within the strictly allotted time until the Hour comes for the emergence of new Manvantaras, or the Ages of Awakening, the Cycles of which are also to be outlined by Periods in which new Times are manifested. As in the great, so in the small — a chain of tests is set forth at the level of every blade of grass. Does not the course of the progressive movement of Time depend largely on us? And does it not come upon evil times when Time encounters us on its path? Perhaps if we happen to present ourselves as a bundle of evil — it might seem that way, but if we serve as a source of good effusions, then meeting us means that good times come for Time as well. Perhaps Time was sent for us from the unknown Empyreal Worlds, where the Spirit of Immortality abides.

We became mortal, having lost the connecting thread with our stellar spirit, and Eternity is trying to return what we lost over the course of our extended earthly wanderings. Who knows?! Time will tell! For us the main thing is not to go astray, but to keep in step with Time. And may it be our good and faithful companion throughout Eternal Times! Let it be so. Amen.

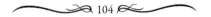

Parable 11

SORROW
AND JOY

nce upon a time Sorrow and Joy happened to run across each other. They were both so astounded by the meeting that they sat down and began to ponder the event. Why had they never met before? Why was it impossible for their paths to cross when they had both been settled on the *terra firma* of the Earth ever since the time of Creation, each concerned every hour about how and where to sow their respective seeds? Sorrow sowed miseries, while Joy cultivated joyous shoots. But where might they have been living? Was it not on the same planet?

"Where have you been dwelling?" asked Joy.

"In the same place you have — in man!" replied Sorrow.

"But if we have had the same abode, how is it that we have not met before?" enquired Joy.

"Because there is no place for me where the currents of Joy fill all space," answered Sorrow. "Just like the Snow Queen, I begin to melt as soon as I fall under the influence of the sunny and happy fires of Joy — evidently that is why I have avoided meeting with you all this time. After all, like every creation of Nature, I, too, have an instinct for self-preservation. But millennia of wanderings around the world have left their mark upon me. And perhaps I am not the same Sorrow I was in the beginning. Something has changed in me. I have been greatly yearning to meet with Joy!"

"Well, I am extremely glad to meet with you!" said Joy and poured the breath of the Sun's rays over Sorrow.

"Finally we did it!" responded Sorrow. "Even though I avoided direct encounters, I was still searching for you, because, like every creation of Life, I wanted someone to be glad to see me as well. Nobody has ever waited for me, and whenever I approached, people would always chase me away. And each time, in trying to get rid of me, they would commit acts that led to even greater misfortunes. I will tell you frankly: I have been flourishing on the Earth for a long, long time. Entire nations would call upon me, but not for themselves — they would send me

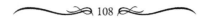

to neighbouring countries, and these, in turn, would sic me upon the heads of *their* enemies. I never knew even a moment of rest, serving the Human Race as a weapon — a Human Race divided, embittered, always envying other people's good."

"People have changed!" Joy enthusiastically noted.

"Yes..." Sorrow thoughtfully agreed. "They are constantly calling for you! Maybe they are tired of living under my control. Maybe they realize that when they wish misery upon others, they primarily attract it to themselves. But such is the Law: *Do not wish for others what you do not wish for yourself!* I have lost my power over human minds." Sorrow concluded.

"So that is where you have been living!" exclaimed Joy. "That is why we never met, because we were dwelling in different spheres. After all, my abode has been the human heart!"

"Of course, the human mind is not the ideal haven!" said Sorrow. "It is too dualistic and lives more according to the Law of Negation of

Negations. First it wants one thing, another time it wants the exact opposite. Frankly speaking, I myself have grown weary of my heavy burden. Perhaps not only the Cup of the world's misery is overflowing, but mine, too, is full beyond measure, and this may be why I have been desiring a meeting with Joy!"

"You have correctly perceived the operation of the Law," said Joy thoughtfully, as though reflecting on what she had just heard. "People have begun to wish each other good, joy, prosperity, and many other things that act as faithful guardians and not allow soothsayers of sorrow to come even close. Certainly, in wishing others joyous days of destiny, they have thereby determined their own, and the grave fate hanging over the entire Human Race has taken on a different coloration, illumined by the sun-reflecting light."

"But, still, how were we able to meet?" Sorrow refused to let up. "After all, even in my quest to meet with you, I still avoided a direct encounter, knowing that it would mean the end of me! Joy and Sorrow cannot be neighbours — they, like the Sun and Moon, never meet together, even though they inhabit the same sky. And the Orb of night simply ceases to exist as soon as the first rays of dawn make their appearance."

"I shall let you in on a secret," confided Joy quietly. "People have begun to listen to their hearts. That is why the mind has retreated to the back burner. More and more they are learning to trust the silent voice of their heart, confident that it will never lead them into misery, for it knows only the path of Joy. And the human mind no longer rebels, now that it has started to calculate the number of misfortunes it is to blame for. Every child of God has sipped enough of the Cup of Sorrow, and experience is an implacable judge. And no reasonable being would ever consciously seek out new miseries when their breast is so markedly scarred by previous wounds and exhausted by misfortune after misfortune."

"So, who brought me into this world then?" desperately questioned Sorrow. "Who felt they had to immerse the entire Human Race in the abyss of hopelessness? After all, does not

everyone, deep inside their soul, yearn for Joy?!
And just look how even I, Sorrow, have longed
for your fires!"

"Do not be sad!" responded Joy. "You see,
if they were unacquainted with Sorrow, people
might not know, too, the healing currents of Joy.
After all, the world is binary, and the mind is
dualistic, and if its negative pole has been overly
emphasized up until now, then the time has
come for it to turn to the positive pole. And so,
it has simply moved from a state of denial to one
of approval. And the all-affirming mind is now
the mouthpiece of the Heart."

"But if the human mind has begun to serve
the heart in this way, does not this mean, too,
that Joy is asserting her control over the former
foundations of Sorrow?"

"If you were looking for me, it means you will
never know sorrow, for there is no sorrow in me,
and I can offer you only what I own, namely, Joy.
And you must realize that you undertook this
quest of yours... not for death, but for life."

"It appears to me that I am at last penetrating

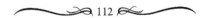

some secret key to understanding myself. I am the companion of the human mind. And if it immerses itself in the heart, then I am obliged to follow, and accept whatever power it recognizes as sovereign over itself."

"This is where our paths crossed," said Joy, "at the Gate of the Heart. Come into my house and live in joy, and you will at once let go of your sorrowful burden!"

"Are you really glad to see me?" Sorrow all at once jumped up and stood face to face with the fire-breathing figure of Joy. "Think of all the sorrow I have caused you, for infinitely long millennia not letting you into my own domain! And what if I suddenly start to flood human hearts with currents of hopelessness, and they become the seedbed of new miseries? Crawling on its belly like a snake, might not a negative thought build a nest and raise countless little vipers, as it did before in the abode of the human mind? How reasonable are you, O Joy of the Heart, in your magnanimity?"

"So genial am I in my generosity that I am

ready to bestow a garment of fire upon you, thanks to which all your rags, all worn out over the long journey of your earthly wanderings, will be instantly incinerated. No one can venture into another's home and impose a routine of one's own, let alone enter my temple or even find its Gate. And if you now appear at my threshold, this is only because you have deliberately been searching for me and following my luminous beacons, even though it meant deviating from your own ways, which were paved with the darkness of despair. And how can I possibly turn a hapless wanderer away from the Gate of Salvation? Joy lives according to the laws of Joy, and so you may experience my warm welcome!"

Suddenly a thought dawned upon Sorrow: "Have not I been serving you? The closer I was to people and the more unchallenged seemed my power over them, the more zealously they were calling for you — Joy! Possibly I, just like the merciless winds, was actually hastening the journey of Noah's Ark towards the shore of salvation? Tell me straight out, have not I been acting

as a servant, competing with my Lord in power?"

"Servants are unknown to me," Joy decisively declared, "for I do not experience joy when communicating with subservient beings, though I do recognize Service as a path consciously chosen by one who has been yearning to stand at my right hand. I am always glad to have a good ally at my side! And, consciously or unconsciously, you *have* done me a good service, for amidst hopeless misery the foundations of the Human Race have been touched by Enlightenment, and it saw a solution by turning to the Heart — the only organ with knowledge of the path to the Empyreal Spheres."

"Well, what you say is after my own heart," Sorrow acknowledged quietly and humbly, and immediately caught himself: "But do I have a heart?"

"Everyone who has reached out to Joy has a heart. Except that there are different kinds of joy — just as there are different kinds of heart. Often people mistake gloating delight for joy. After all, when you come to think about it, jackals and vultures feeding on carrion have hearts as well. And it would be impossible for them to understand the secret meaning of our meeting. After all, they know only one scenario when joy and sorrow meet each other: a predator tightly grasping its prey. A tiger thrusting its fangs into a doe experiences joy, whereas the doe feels only the misery of death... But let us not talk about misery — let it all remain in the past."

"Yes, it is indeed a woeful picture!" sighed Sorrow. "Yet one can understand the predator's situation too — otherwise how could it survive and feed its young?"

"But do we need predators?" queried Joy. "That is the question!"

"But if they cause nothing but sorrow, then hardly!" Sorrow became thoughtful. "So if it were not for me, then there would be no sorrow?" A flash of illumination flitted across the whole essence of whatever manifested itself as misery.

"Absolutely! Where would it come from if you left this world?"

"But I have sown sorrow so solidly throughout the earthly world!"

"Nevertheless, sprouts always reach out towards the Sun, and those which are about to sprout, will they not reach out to you by the force of magnetic attraction? You are their kind of orb. Indeed, people say: 'Troubles never come alone.' Or: 'One misfortune comes on the heels of another.' Such is the Law of Attraction: all things consonant with each other aspire to merge together."

"But how could we, being so different from each other, possibly meet together — two essences, serving as the source of Joys and sorrows?"

"Extremes do come together — and this is a rule, too. They represent two forces, practically equivalent values, often representing the two poles of a particular unified conglomeration. This essence becomes divided, as it were, within itself, eliciting both the highest and the lowest sounds. Thus, stretched apart in time and space, the two focuses, marked by a plus and a minus sign, begin to serve as a special kind of magnet which attracts to itself, so to speak, both the best and worst, in accordance with the designated signs. Then, if one turns out to have superior strength, it simply absorbs the other..."

"Oh, that is what is called Evolution!" Sorrow impatiently interrupted. "I know it is something hidden within you, and it is stronger than you. And no matter how hard you try to insist on your own position, it erupts from deep within your depths, forcing you to turn off the well-trodden paths and make your way through dense thickets, leading straight towards an unknown goal!" At this point Sorrow became confused and silent, apparently listening to some mysterious process taking place within.

And right there a quiet joy was ripening. It was rising as a fragile little sprout, all iridescent with emerald facets. Slowly, carefully — but confidently — the sprout, as though sheltered in closed palms, brought forth a small bud that was ready to unfold all its petals towards the Sun of Life. Yes, the world is indeed binary, and even Sorrow, having experienced so much misery in the course of his mournful way, still found the strength within himself to strive to attain the focus of Joy.

And how could it be otherwise? After all, this world was created by the Supreme Charter, whose basis is formed by the currents of Joy. And how can you possibly get away from her, being already embraced by her fervent arms which so tenderly warm the soul? Indeed, Sorrow has not only a heart but also a soul if he stands still so sweetly, caressed by the gentle currents of his Lord. O how joyful is this Service, where no one chases you away, where you are always welcome. And the only thing that remains to wish for is: *Let it last forever...* And so it will, indeed! Amen.

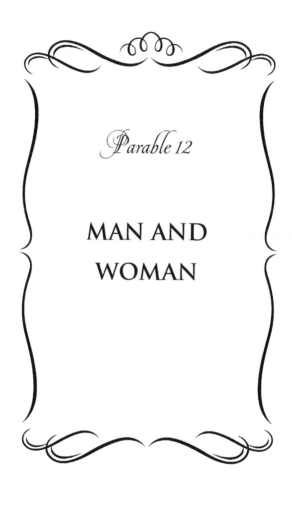

Parable 12

MAN AND
WOMAN

When did the history of the relations of Man and Woman begin? Did anyone write it down, expanding on the pages of the ancient chronicles? Oh, how many wonderful pictures would appear before our gaze, coming to life in all their many colours, if suddenly someone found a pile of decaying manuscripts, stored for the time being in secure hiding-places until the world might be ready to comprehend the secret essence of Man's relation to Woman and Woman's relation to Man.

Indeed, this story began a long, long time ago — one could say: before the Earth even existed, though Man and Woman already existed! They lived beyond the borders of our Universe — after all, it is no longer a secret for anyone that such outer spheres, termed Infinity, conceal myriads of Universes within themselves. And it is not surprising that human Earth-dwellers know nothing of them, since, in comparison with the inhabitants of other worlds, they are yet immature little children, even when it comes to knowing their own selves. Hence the "chroniclers" of the Ethereal Spheres decided to draw Earth-dwellers' attention to the unwritten pages of their history which have been so mindlessly lost on that small planet.

Once upon a time there lived Man and Woman in the unknown depths of the Stellar Ocean. They were so inseparable that they almost constituted a single, indivisible essence. And the strength of their mutual attraction, ever increasing day by day, was so beautiful that it was pouring over into a fanciful spectacle of stellar light. Of course, those who watched them from the level of other planets simply saw a star ablaze with iridescent florescence. They breathed each other's Fire — this Man and Woman — and so each of them wanted to give as much light-infused nourishment to each other as possible. After all, they had been created in the image and likeness of God, and God is a "consuming Fire." And what can supply a greater flame than Love?! Yes, it was she whom they breathed — Love herself, generously nourishing them with the currents of life, protecting them through all the paths of progression. Of course, just like any planet, every star has its orbit traversing the depths of the Stellar Ocean. Thus, the single light-bearing essence formed by the union of Man and Woman was moving towards a destiny unknown, as outlined in fiery turns by the Hand of Lady Love herself. It was as though she were testing their strength in pursuit of goals known only to her.

What do you think, might a star have its own guiding star? As for Man, he calls Woman his lodestar and, as for Woman, obviously, her guiding star will be the Man towards whom her trembling heart is drawn. But if we examine the union represented by their merging, then, surely, their only guiding star will be... *Love*. So they strive towards Love, endeavouring to comprehend the incomprehensible and reach the unreachable. No matter how many secret pages we uncover — pages inscribed by tales of loving hearts — Love will still remain a Mystery. And is there someone who has had enough of Love? Human beings, as rational creatures, always want to be loved more.

Yes, no matter how much we are loved, we always seem to lack the feelings experienced by those who love us. And if the fire of a lamp is fuelled by adding oil, does not our Love, too, depend upon those to whom it is expressed? What if the flame of hopes for a reciprocal feeling ceases to burn, once we notice that the object of our desires is absolutely indifferent to us? But if we show coldness towards those who really harbour a heartfelt feeling towards us, are not we acting pretty much as a north wind, blowing out someone's little fire with our icy breath? But if this fire has been lit by the hand of Love, do not we commit a crime by killing a life-bearing seed in the bud? Who is responsible for the Love living not only in our breast but also in the hearts of all those who are close to us — or even those at a distance? What will happen to those who have beheld the guiding star in us? And what will happen to us if the light of our chosen star — the goal of our journey — should suddenly go out? How do we avoid making a mistake and getting carried away with the radiance of another star which is following its own lodestar? After all, everyone has their individual star — the only one that shines just for them.

Myriads of stars are scattered throughout the Ocean of Eternity. And it is just possible that every Orb includes within itself the two Fires joined together — the Great Masculine and the Great Feminine Principles. Who has been able to peer into the Holy of Holies and give us a reliable report as to where one can find that source through which Man and Woman are brought into the world? Perchance, the Universe itself serves as a kind of womb, bearing within itself the Divine Fruit? And, being subject to laws unknown, it begets the unified essence we know as Man and Woman. After all, the Earth is binary in its essence, and so they cannot arrive here already united together. Perhaps we would come closer to comprehending yet another page of the great Mystery if we could see at least one example showing the union of Man and Woman, living by each other's breath and constituting a single Orb, nourishing each other with the effusive Fire of

Love. Possibly they would be seen as a lodestar to Earth-dwellers who have never known unity, even when merged together within the so-called union of marriage. People, like stellar deposits, are scattered throughout the Earth, but they are unacquainted with the great peace of the stars, for they represent but half of their essence, and therefore they constantly traipse about creation in an eternal quest for a being that will allow them to experience their wholeness.

The Mystery of the origin of Man and Woman will never be solved on the Earth, if one's gaze is not directed into the depths of the Stellar Ocean. But note that the progressive orbit of our familiar Orb has been approaching our planet. And stellar Man has given his hand to Woman, offering to walk with her on a green carpet dappled with petals of exotic flowers. So, like a child leaving the maternal womb at the time appointed, Man and Woman have stepped out of the House of their light-giving Spirit. And all at once people on the Earth notice a falling star. "Someone is born!" they exclaim and, of course, they are right. And how can they still be considered as a celestial orb when the Man and Woman constituting its light have left the dome of the sky and set their feet upon the "*terra firma*" of the Earth? However, the planet, even though a dwarf star, was in the germinative state of its development, and so implacable guards stood at its Gate, letting in only those who possessed currents consonant with the planet itself. Thus both Man and Woman had to dim the light of their own resplendence. They seemed to lose the halo of their stellar rays and immerse themselves in the gloom. Indeed, it could not be otherwise, since night practically reigned supreme in the surrounding spheres, and the planet still had but a vague idea of what constituted Day, manifest in the glowing zenith of the solar rays. But where was the green carpet, dappled with exotic flowers? It turned out to be an island, wisely prepared by the hands of Lady Love for the children under her care.

Indeed, it was Paradise! Stellar couples settled there, and even with their light dimmed, they could not lose sight of each other, because they held on to their unity. They continued to live according to the Law of their own world, for it was implanted in the essence of their internal structure. Love was the source of their existence: they would inhale fiery nourishment and reciprocally exhale, breathing each other's breath. And the light of their radiance, growing stronger with every moment, was seen as dangerous to the nature of the planet itself.

And so the Earth decided to put an end to such phenomena, for she was not ready to serve as a cradle for conceiving stellar beings. She created her own man and woman, attempting to re-create forms out of dust and ashes, as similar as possible to stellar beings. But they resembled, rather, lumps of mud, and the planet destroyed one form after another, until she managed to create something more or less suitable for life. But she turned out to be too short-lived in respect to the existence of her creations, composed as they were of perishable matter. So, the small planet called upon her elder brethren, orbs of the first magnitude, for help in the creation of Man and Woman in the image and likeness of the stars. Yet, were not the Forces which conceived entire Universes, already aware of that, and was not this the reason why, at the formative dawn of the planet, a stellar dwarf, celestial couples were already stepping upon her "*terra firma*"? But the Earth herself was not taken by surprise, as she had wisely prepared a blissful place for her kind helpers, which one could truly call a Paradise of the Earth.

So, All-Giving Love blessed them by her generous hand for their faraway journey, immersing the stellar beings in an earthly vale of tears and misery. And nourished with each other's fire, Man and Woman set out along the orbits of progression, along the life paths prepared for them by Destiny in the image of Love, who tested the strength of their "feelings." And because they lived by each other's eternal breath, their nature included a particle of the opposite principle. And even though "cleft" in two, they preserved the currents of their other half. Woman never ceased being a woman, even as the bearer of masculine qualities, just as Man never lost the keynote of the Great Masculine Principle, even if he was permeated with a multitude of properties truly feminine in nature. They were called upon to traverse the entire planet, descending the rungs of density and, after reaching the lowest point of material coagulation, to ascend once more to their original position. And they were to make their way amidst the Kingdom called Human.

At first glance, the test conditions might seem terribly cruel, for they were to part from the one from whom they had never been separated even for an instant as they trod their luminous path through the Ocean of Eternity. Moreover, they were to raise a creature composed of earthly dust and ashes to the place formerly occupied by their lodestar! But, firm in the knowledge that every test has its limits, Man and Woman set off on their long journey. Humbly bowing their heads before the Supreme Will of Love, each of them followed their own path in the tracks of their guiding star, who wished to lead them precisely along such a path, deflecting the orbit of progression to penetrate the dense throngs of humankind. Thus, stellar and earthly Man and Woman mingled on the petrified *terra firma*, like leaves plucked from the crown of the trees on which they had grown and, driven by gusty winds, they found shelter where most often a stumbling-block lay, over which it was difficult to step — as it was thus foreordained for them by the destiny of the Earth. And the latter, of course, had no idea as to what All-Giving Love might be, for it served dust and ashes.

So Man and Woman merged together, only the former was woven from stellar light, while she who shared a bed with him was created from perishable currents. He began to breathe in what she breathed out, filling himself with mortal breath, because she nourished herself on particles permeated with the spirit of decay. He tried to infuse his light into her, endowing her with the nourishment of Fire, but she did not feel a need for it. But could he possibly reproach her for that? After all, at the level of the material from which she was created, fire was not only not needed, but might even be dangerous. If he increased the intensity of the flame, he might well incinerate the earthly tissue of which she was composed. And Man, now permeated with dust and ashes, began to dim his fires even more, in an attempt to find the key to the secret mechanisms that empowered the life-currents of mortal beings. And Man kept descending lower and lower until he reached the very nadir of the orbit of his own progression, as designated by the Hand of All-Giving Love. And at this point he was to begin following the upward steps.

But now it seemed as though leaden weights were shackling his whole body. Perhaps, he had already taken root in the earthly soil and the mortal body formed of dust and ashes was now being drawn towards food permeated with the spirit of decay, unaware of its need of fiery ingredients? Where should he go, what should he aspire to, if he could not see the light of his guiding star either on the Earth or in Heaven? Was not that an impasse? But surely she who led him here, having set out the invisible orbit through the thickets of the densest spheres, must have had a secret goal?! Was it Love?! Even she seemed to have abandoned him. There were two of them, as always — Man and Woman — but both now experienced feelings of loneliness. Indeed, the earthly bed only intensified the spirit of alienation through brief instants of unification, affirming that they would never merge for eternity.

Why have Man and Woman undertaken such a strange journey? They may seem to be different beings, but at the same time they have a common need, namely *Love*! And regardless of whether they are earthly or heavenly beings, they seem to be seeking the same thing in each other... *Love*. Still, each will have their own understanding of Love: some seek it for themselves, others for someone else. And herein lies the secret meaning of the test vouchsafed by Lady Love. She is the eternal source, nourishing those under her care with food of Fire, and she would like to see all life in the world as an example similar to herself. And so she marches along stellar orbits in the image of Man and Woman, stepping where no human

being has ever set foot. Man and Woman —
these are the two poles of a single Essence, named
Love! And may they be united and inseparable
through ages eternal! Let it be so! Amen.

*A parable is contained in a parable, just as in us:
Woman in Man and Man in Woman. And if Love
lives within us, we shall always be able to maintain
our integrity, even after thousands of centuries, as
we head towards the one with whom we are destined to continue an everlasting path joining us
together. Perchance, then, someone at some time
will compile the pages of chronicles, elucidating the
history of the Love of Humanity, which will rise to
the Heavens as brightly shining stars in an attempt
to comprehend the great Mystery — the Mystery of
the Unity and Indivisibility of Man and Woman,
who continue to tread their Stellar Path as they
reach beyond the limits of infinite new Eternities.*

About the Author

Zinovia Dushkova, Ph.D., is a Russian author, poet, philosopher, historian, and traveller. She has been honoured with a number of awards, prizes, and commendations for her contribution to the spiritual development of society, and for excellence in the domain of scientific research into the ecology of consciousness. She is a Fellow of the European Academy of Natural Sciences and the European Scientific Society, both based in Hanover, Germany.

A seeker of ancient truths, Dr. Dushkova has always strived to find only one thing: Love. She has engaged in research in Asia, Africa, Europe, and North America for more than twenty years, acquiring the secret wisdom underlying all known religions and philosophies. On her way, lying across mountains and deserts, she has stayed at numerous sanctuaries of various peoples. These include: widely known Buddhist monasteries, following the Mahayana and Vajrayana philosophies, such as Ganden, Drepung, Sera, the famous Moru, dedicated to studying the profound mysteries of Buddhist mysticism, as well as Hindu temples of Vishnu, Shiva, Krishna, and other Saints. However, Dr. Dushkova has also stayed at remote monasteries and secret Abodes hidden in mountains, deserts, and caves in Tibet, Mongolia, Nepal, and India, which cannot be described in any detail. After all, these are the places which have preserved the oldest sacred scrolls and manuscripts, such as the secret *Book of Dzyan*, from which her famous predecessors in esoteric philosophy, Helena Blavatsky and Helena Roerich, obtained their own wisdom.

As a result of the rich experience of studying sacred texts and communication with wise monks and hermits, since 1997 nearly forty works by Dr. Dushkova have been published in Russia, Ukraine, Moldova, and France. These works are all of a spiritual nature, having been recorded during her travels in the Himalayas, the Karakorum, the Nilgiri, the Gobi Desert, the Pyrenees, and beyond. They reflect a neat synthesis of science, religion, history, and philosophy. Underlying Dr. Dushkova's poetry and prose, her fairy tales and legends, is a worldview full of wisdom and the cultural heritage of both the East and the West.

Visit the author's official website and sign up for a newsletter at:
www.dushkova.com/en

Follow the author at:
www.facebook.com/ZinoviaDushkova
www.twitter.com/ZinoviaDushkova
www.goodreads.com/ZinoviaDushkova

THE BOOK OF SECRET WISDOM

A million years ago, the Great Masters of Wisdom recorded a mysterious manuscript widely known as the *Book of Dzyan* — a Tibetan name meaning the *Book of Secret Wisdom*. Written in a language unfamiliar to modern philology, called *Senzar*, this oldest book in the world has served as the source of every ancient religion, philosophy, and science.

The Masters stored it in the legendary realm of Shambhala, each century admitting only a few chosen ones to read some of its pages. Now a new excerpt, consisting of twelve stanzas and supplemented with exclusive material, is published in English for the first time. Reading through the pages of this work, you will be able to trace the whole course of the spiritual evolution of humanity and our Earth beyond Time and Space.

THE TEACHING OF THE HEART

*I*n 1997, on the statue of Buddha in South Korea, for the first time in 3,000 years, a sacred flower blossomed — the *udumbara*, which is now to be found all over the world.

According to Buddhist scriptures, it heralds the approaching Advent of the Greatest Teacher, the Lord of the legendary kingdom of Shambhala hidden in the Himalayas. He is Maitreya for some, Christ for others, and the Mahdi for many more: He is the promised Messiah of all religions.

The Teaching of the Heart series invites you to embark on a fascinating spiritual journey together with the Great Lord of Shambhala. He will lead you along the path of the supreme wisdom that will transform not only your own life, but also the whole world.

Made in the USA
Middletown, DE
26 May 2021